Climate Crisis

A Plan to Prevent Future Flooding

By
Acie Cargill

Published by Acie Cargill

aciecargill@gmail.com

http://aciecargill.com

ISBN: 9781080856022

Imprint: Independently published

Formatted - Brenda Van Niekerk

brenda@triomarketers.com

Website Design - Brenda Van Niekerk

http://triomarketers.com

Synopsis

There is climate change in this world. A climate crisis. The entire Earth is affected and some places worse than others. What about the Mississippi River flooding? It was bad this year and may be worse next year and every year from now on unless we make major changes in our abuse of the planet. Rain, rain, and more rain. And it is still going on. Some parts of the Earth are affected by extreme heat and droughts. Severe weather like hurricanes. Melting of our polar ice caps. The high water in the Mississippi River also affects the Delta where it enters the Gulf of Mexico. This area was where fish and shrimp had their young, but this year it is not happening because of the high water in the Mississippi. I am proposing a plan here to avoid the Mississippi flooding.

The idea is to get the excess water out of the Mississippi basin and send it to where it is desperately needed out West. We could dig a huge canal for thousands of miles and spend many billions of dollars or it would be much easier to reverse the flow of some rivers flowing into the Mississippi, for instance the Arkansas River, and cause that water to flow west instead. The Arkansas River joins with the Canadian River and could flow through Oklahoma where the water is needed and at present the Canadian River is almost dry in some places.

From there, the water could be routed into New Mexico and even Arizona through some of the nearly dry river beds. The water could be used for agricultural purposes and human consumption and for nature and wildlife. Bring the desert to life with the water from the Mississippi that otherwise is causing massive destruction from flooding almost every year. The key is the reversal of the water flow in the rivers. An example of flow reversal is the Chicago River that was reversed to carry sewage away from Lake Michigan. It can be done and large amounts of water can be routed to the West where it is needed

About the Author

Acie Cargill is a poet, a songwriter, and a prose writer. He studied poetry with USA Poet Laureate Mark Strand and Illinois Poet Laureate Gwendolyn Brooks. He studied novel writing with Thomas Berger, who wrote Little Big Man (that Arthur Penn made into a movie with Dustin Hoffman in the lead role). Cargill also studied journalism with instructor Jean Daily. His work is a synthesis of all these styles.

He is a member of American Mensa and formerly Edited the Mensa Journal of Poetry. He also is a member of the Grammy Association, and The US Quill and Scroll Society.

Cargill is a vegetarian, a former holistic physician, a musical performer on a variety of instruments, an environmental activist, a lecturer, medical reviewer, a lover, and a seer.

Website

http://aciecargill.com

Contact

aciecargill@gmail.com

Other Books Written by the Author:

Puerto Rico

Aberrations

Chronicles

Terrorism

Modern Love

Ends and odds

Illiana: The Border Area Between Illinois and Indiana

Pullman

Che and Fidel - A Reading Play of the Cuban Revolution

Celia Sanchez - A Play of the Cuban Revolution

Paschke - A Play

Gwendolyn Brooks: A Play

Rasputin - A Play

Nietzsche - A Play

Bob Dylan, The Early Years - A Musical Play

Michael Jackson - A Play

Einstein - A Biographical Play

El Chapo - A Play In 3 Acts

Raisins and Roaches - A Three Month Diary of a Crack Addict

Susan B. Anthony - A Biographical Play

Kankakee

Harriet Tubman - A Biographical Play

Tesla - A Biographical Play

Vegan Saint - A Play in 3 Acts

Martin Luther King, Jr - A Play

Great Migration: A Play in 3 Acts

George Pullman - A Play in Three Acts

Frederick Douglass - A Biographical Play

Freud - A Biographical Play in 3 Acts

The Underground Railroad - An Educational Play

Payton, Jordan, Ali - A Biographical Play

Mr. Nobody - A Play

The Kid From Left Field - A Play

Puerto Rico, A Dream of Independence - A Play in 3 Acts

Crack Madness - A Monologue Play

Johnny Appleseed - A Family Play

Dr. Jekll and Mr. Hyde - A Modernized Play

Obama - Obama - A Play In 3 Acts

Will Rogers - A Biographical Monologue

Merle Haggard - A Biographical Monologue

Mother Teresa - A Biographical Monologue

Gwendolyn Brooks - A Biographical Monologue

Love Life of Susan B. Anthony - A Monologue Play

Sojourner Truth - A Biographical Monologue plus Narrator

Harriet Tubman and The Underground Railroad - A Play

Helen Keller, Words and Wisdom - A Biographical Play

Eugene Debs and the 1894 Pullman Strike - A Play

The Rising - A Play

Walt Disney - A Biographical One Act Play

The Experiments of Dr. Victor Frankenstein - A Play - Based on the novel by Mary Shelley

Karl Marx - A One Act Play

Martin Luther at The Diet of Worms - A One Act Play

Martin Luther King: Monologue and Narrator Play

Frederick Douglass - Monologue and Narrator Play

Kaepernick - A One Act Play

Settling South Holland - A Play In 2 Acts

Kaepernick - A Full-Length Play

My Son Died From An Overdose - A Play

Overdose - A One Act Play

Always a Marine First

Erotic Muslim Polygamy

George Dolton's Bridge to Freedom Underground Railroad - A One-Act Play

Greta Thunberg - A One-Act Play About Climate Change

A Brief History of the Philippines

Goat With No Horns - Voodoo Cannibals in Haiti

Johnny Cash - Monologue Play

Muhammad Words Of Wisdom

Jesus Words Of Wisdom

Bob Hope - Biographical Monologue

The Cargills of Graves County, Ky

Keith Raniere and the NXIVM Sex Club

Words of Wisdom – Native Americans, Ancient Greeks, Buddha and African-Americans

Words of Wisdom – Mark Twain, Benjamin Franklin, Shakespeare and Solomon

The Trial of Eddie Gallagher, Navy SEAL

There is climate change in this world. A climate crisis. The entire Earth is affected and some places worse than others. What about the Mississippi River flooding? It was bad this year and may be worse next year and every year from now on unless we make major changes in our abuse of the planet. Rain, rain, and more rain. And it is still going on. Some parts of the Earth are affected by extreme heat and droughts. Severe weather like hurricanes. Melting of our polar ice caps. The high water in the Mississippi River also affects the Delta where it enters the Gulf of Mexico. This rea was where fish and shrimp had their young, but this year it is not happening because of the high water in the Mississippi. I am going to propose a plan to avoid the Mississippi flooding.

The idea is to get the excess water out of the Mississippi basin and send it to where it is desperately needed out West. We could dig a huge canal for thousands of miles and spend many billions of dollars or it would be much easier to reverse the flow of some rivers flowing into the Mississippi, for instance the Arkansas River, and cause that water to flow west instead. The Arkansas River joins with the Canadian River and could flow through Oklahoma where the water is needed and at present the Canadian River is almost dry in some places.

From there, the water could be routed into New Mexico and even Arizona through some of the nearly dry river beds. The water could be used for agricultural purposes and human consumption and for nature and wildlife. Bring the desert to life with the water from the Mississippi that otherwise is causing massive destruction from flooding almost every year. The key is the reversal of the water flow in the rivers. An example of flow reversal is the Chicago River that was reversed to carry sewage away from Lake Michigan. It can be done and large amounts of water can be routed to the West where it is needed.

I am no engineer and no hydrologist. I am just using logic and making suggestions as to what can be done. Not how to do it. That is for someone else. I can see that certain rivers now flowing into the Mississippi can be reversed and draw water out of the Mississippi to relieve flooding and make life better for those people living along the banks of this great river. There is so much water flowing in the Mississippi that drawing some of it off and sending it west will not damage the Mississippi itself. Naturally there will be people who resent any kind of changes. There always is, but if their home area has been flooded, they will probably be conducive to any means of reducing these flood waters. With the climate crisis expected to worsen, something must be done.

The Chicago River is fairly large. A lot of water. And deep. Around the year1900, sanitary engineers had to do something because the sewage was flowing into Lake Michigan and causing many thousands of terrible deaths from sewage-borne diseases like typhoid fever and cholera. Moving the intake s for the drinking water farther out into the lake helped but if there was a big storm, the drinking water again became tainted with disease causing microbes. Reversing the flow of the river was not an easy job, but it was absolutely necessary.

A canal 28 miles long was dug and that was a big job in those days with the primitive digging methods. There also had to be locks built to keep everything in balance and some dams to hold back the river water until the canal was ready to receive the water. Then the dams were opened and the water flowed rapidly into the canal and into the Des Plaines River and then the Illinois River and then the Mississippi River. The Chicago River was reversed in its flow and the water came out of Lake Michigan and into the Sanitary and Ship Canal and Chicago had saved it's population from the devastation of disease. The canal also provided a highway for barge and ship traffic from the Mississippi and Gulf of Mexico to Lake Michigan and the St. Lawrence seaway and the Atlantic Ocean. Both ways. Another canal called the Cal-Sag Canal, was built on the South Side of Chicago connecting the Illinois River with the industrial areas along the Calumet Rivers.

Chicago's wastes and sewage are now processed and disinfected before being sent down the rivers and canals. The towns and cities downriver from Chicago are required to disinfect the water for their municipal water supplies, but that was going to be necessary anyway. A lot of cities and towns along the rivers were dumping raw sewage into the rivers and Chicago was not the only source of sewage and eventually Chicago's sewage was processed before being released.

So what does all that mean? Rivers now flowing into the Mississippi and for that matter, the Missouri River and Ohio River can be reversed and rerouted if necessary to prevent the destructive flooding that will probably accompany the heavy rains associated with the climate crisis. If you are living near the Arkansas River, for example, you probably would not notice much difference in your life with the water flowing out of the Mississippi instead of into it, but it would make a big difference to the parched areas of the West that could really use the water.

Just think of the crops and natural areas being benefitted as well as creating a surplus of water in the towns along the affected rivers. It might be necessary to dig some connecting canals and dams to hold back the water until it is ready to be reversed. There would be some costs involved naturally, but think of the huge costs saved to the areas that were getting flooded.

Naturally there would be some changes in the fish and flora with the extra water flowing in from the Mississippi. Wouldn't the changes be worth it to rejuvenate the drier areas out West? There would be changes. A lot of people do not like any changes, no matter how beneficial or necessary. Many people like everything left just the way it occurs naturally. I think they should be overruled for the benefits of the river reversals, not the least of which is the alleviation of flooded cities, towns, and homes. People had better get used to changes. Our world will never be the same as it was with all the carbon fuel emissions going into the atmosphere and changing our climate.

How many people in the world are willing to make changes and sacrifices in their personal lives and power consumption. It is not just in the United States although we are one of the worst abusers. Families have multiple gas devouring cars and use huge amounts of personal electric consumption. Every room in their massive homes have air conditioners with entertainment centers with televisions, sound systems, video games, and computers. Without all this, the people in the family will feel deprived and might even express their animosity to the head of the household. It will not be easy to cut our wasteful consumption in America.

Consumption equates to emissions with the possible exception of the minority of homeowners using renewable energy sources such as solar, wind, and hydro. Most of us are dependent on carbon consumption for our energy needs. Or possibly nuclear which has dangers and disadvantages of its own. And there is not much we can do about it if we want to take part to an extent in the modern world. Everyone could become more conscious of their carbon footprint and that includes our food habits which are usually wasteful and cruel. Wasteful of energy and actually wasteful of the food itself.

Possibly the beginning of trying as individual to be more climate conscious would be to evaluate our diets. Our current majority meat based diet is very inefficient and polluting. Our soils and fuels are used to grow grain to feed to animals. It would take only a small percentage of the land and fuel and human resources if we ate the grains and vegetables ourselves. Just cutting the American meat consumption in half would provide enough extra food that there would be no hunger anywhere in the world and maybe many of the wild animals becoming extinct from hunting for food by starving natives would be saved.

Less of the rainforest would have to be destroyed for growing food when we could send our excess food to those countries. The rainforests were always the great savior of this planet. All that vegetation would absorb the much of the carbon in our emissions and it would be converted and stored as wood instead of going into the atmosphere to cause global warming and the myriad of other climate changes and imbalances caused by the warming.

Will the people of the world, especially Americans take the steps necessary to drastically slow carbon emissions and the ensuing global warming? It is doubtful because people are basically selfish and unwilling to make any sacrifices in their lifestyles. They think to "let others make changes in their lifestyles but not me." They don't want any changes in their consumption. They are concerned only about their lifetimes and the future be damned. Let the people in the future figure out what can be done and do it then. But for now, people want their lifestyles left as they are and their increasing consumption unimpeded.

Reverse the flow on some rivers flowing into the Mississippi River and maybe the Missouri River and send the water to the dry areas out West. They are going to only get drier with the ensuing climate crisis. I don't know which rivers are the best candidates. That is for water engineers to study and decide. I just see the need and the solution. It will cost some money and some work, but really anything that benefits the world takes some effort and funds. The Mississippi River has way too much water and it seems like it is only going to get worse as time goes on with this climate crisis. Bring the water to where it is needed. Dig canals or pipelines if necessary or just reverse the flow of some rivers to carry the excess water from the Mississippi to areas where it is needed.